Joseph Bedell

A Tour Through the Western States

Joseph Bedell

A Tour Through the Western States

ISBN/EAN: 9783337320973

Printed in Europe, USA, Canada, Australia, Japan

Cover: Foto ©Andreas Hilbeck / pixelio.de

More available books at **www.hansebooks.com**

A TOUR

THROUGH THE

𝔚𝔢𝔰𝔱𝔢𝔯𝔫 𝔖𝔱𝔞𝔱𝔢𝔰,

BY

J. BEDELL.

LONG ISLAND CITY:
PRINTED AT THE "STAR" BOOK & JOB PRINTING OFFICE.
1867.

A TOUR THROUGH THE WEST.

In the good olden times when our forefathers were boys, the chimney corner was a sacred
abiding place for its inmates, undisturbed by
the selfish ambition of wealth and pride, pure,
honest-hearted men, happy and contented, seldom venturing over the sill door or beyond the
bounds of their own farms. If the alphabet
was not learned by the children, the parents
gave themselves no trouble about such trifling
things, country district schools being the highest limits of education. The old slow coach,
and mud sill wagons, with the entire absence
of springs, decorated with an old arm chair,
on the Sabbath day, wending its way to church,
was some of the conditions and facilities of
getting through the world in the days in which
our forefathers lived. During the early settle-
ment of the western states, the condition and
facilities of the country was but little known
to the masses of the people in the eastern states.
To emigrate one or two thousand miles in the

interior of a newly settled country seemed almost like madness on the part of the participant of the expedition.

I had subscribed to the purchase of lands in the State of Illinois, in anticipation of reaping a golden harvest in connection with a desire to see the world, I risked the chances of an expedition through the western States, bidding adieu to the land that gave me birth, and all that was near and dear to me, with a heavy heart and tearful eye, was the scene of my parting farewell.

So loth we part from all we love,
From all the links that bind us,
So turn our hearts, as we rove,
To those we have left behind us.

I left the great metropolis, the city of New York, on the thirteenth day of September, 1836, by the Amboy route; at six o'clock in the evening we arrived at Philadelphia, that good old Quaker city, renowned for historical events. The old State house where our forefathers signed the Declaration of Independence, which gave us birth to the best Institutions and the finest country that the sun ever shone upon, is an object of deep interest. The United States mint, the Gerard College, and the Schuylkill water works are objects of interest for the stranger to visit. The city is located upon a level surface, containing a large area of ground, only second to New York in size and population; the buildings are chiefly composed of brick, of fine architectural style; the streets are laid out in regular blocks, wide and spacious, well adapted for the accommodation of public travel, containing several fine parks, bounded on the east by the Delaware river, full of historical reminiscences, over which the father of our country, that noble patriot, GEORGE WASHINGTON, crossed under unfavorable auspices, through ice bergs with his brave band of soldiers to intercept the enemy, are events which will be handed down to future posterity. We left Philadelphia at one o'clock in the afternoon by railroad for Columbia, a distance of eighty miles, passing through a fine farming section of country, well represented with the peasantry of German settlements, Lancaster being the finest and largest city on the route, the cars gliding along speedily to the terminus of the road, scarcely having time to prepare our budget for transit. The lowback car brought up the heavy baggage; the confusion of transportation from the cars to the boat, requiring a good pair of eyes with an additional mirror to keep watch of its safe transition.

Arriving at Columbia, we took the regular packet line of canal boats for Pittsburg, a distance of three hundred and eighteen miles. The canal boats are usually propelled by horses or mules, rendering our passage slow and tedious, the large number of locks causing much detention, and the tormenting bridges, the narrow births and cramped-up cabins rendering such a journey undesirable and discomforting, but as steam power and electricity had not attained to its highest degree of perfection, we were resolved to submit to the force of circumstances without grumbling, with a consoling thought that there is a compensating sweet for every bitter in the world. We lived sumptuously, and the passengers, seemingly, strove to make themselves pleasant and agreeable; the social chit-chats, the vocal and instrumental music echoing through the forest, over hill and dale in the gleam of moonlight, are events not soon to be forgotten—and the landscape possessing a great variety of scenery, the beautiful foliage of the forest trees, the level plain, lofty mountains, rugged rocks, villages, lakes and rivers, the humble cot and fine farms contributing to make up a picturesque scene, and, indeed, the landscape between Philadelphia and Pittsburg by the canal route, can scarcely be surpassed in any section of country.

Arriving at the foot of the Alleghany mountains, the ascent of two or three thousand feet was attained by the means of railroad cars, drawn up an inclined plane by stationary steam power, located at certain distances, by the means of a large rope attached to the cars. This was indeed a novel scene, creating some degree of timidity among the passengers. By slow degrees we arrived at the summit of the mountain in safety, and within a brief period of time we arrived at the summit house.— Breakfast being prepared, a large number of hungry persons rushed around the table without much ceremony, helping themselves with a hearty good will to a hasty plate of soup, when the bell rang, and the word sounding through the hall, " all on board," created some degree of excitement. A scramble for cloaks, coats and hats—not a spare moment left—and the cars are off. In our plight of haste, some selfish fellow helped himself to a hind leg of a chicken, to dissect at his leisure moments.— Shortly after leaving the hotel the cars passed over a stone bridge (a splendid piece of masonry) at an elevation of eighty feet above the fearful precipice beneath. Within a brief period of time, we entered the mouth of a tunnel eight hundred feet long; a damp, dark looking place, but we only had a few moments for reflection before we came out at the other end, seemingly as if our fiery steed, the iron horse, was bent upon a spree, by the rate of speed we had made. We descended to the foot of the mountain at Johnstown, being a distance of thirty-seven miles by railroad across the mountain. Here we took passage in our old conveyance, the canal boats. During our passage between Johnstown and Pittsburg, we passed through a tunnel nine hundred feet long, with the canal boat and horses attached, at twelve o'clock at night, by lamp lights suspended on the walls of the tunnel, rendering the scene peculiarly interesting. After experiencing a slow tedious voyage for several days and nights, we arrived at Pittsburg, situated at the confluence of three rivers—the Monongahela, Alleghany, and Ohio, the city being a dark, smoky looking place, well represented with manufactories, being convenient to the coal mines, it is used for all convenient purposes. My attention was attracted by the large number of coal cars on the opposite side of the river, passing up and down the mountain, dumping their loads at its base. Owing to the low stage of water in the Ohio river, instituted the necessity of our re· maining at this place for a period of two or three days, a refreshing shower causing the water to rise, enabling us to take passage in a flat-bottom, high-pressure steamer with a wheel in the stern, resembling the old fashioned grist mill wheels, a novelty to those not accustomed to witnessing such a craft; and now we are truly sailing upon the river Ohio, puffing of steam freely, the revolutions of the wheel creating a sort of chills and fever shaking—a frail bark in comparison to our North and East riv· er passenger steamers. Pittsburg, Wheeling, Louisville, and Cincinnati being the largest and most important commercial cities upon the banks of the Ohio river, including several small towns and villages, but the country being generally thinly populated, for most part heavily timbered, the soil fertile, producing good crops of wheat, and fine specimens of corn—I might say tall corn.

Arriving at Louisville, our further progress

by the river being disputed by a cataract of
rocks and a limited supply of water, we were
obliged to pass through a canal a distance of
two miles, made expressly for the passage of
vessels. The large number of wild pigeons
passing over the river at this place attracted
our special attention. Arriving at Cincinnati,
I was favorably impressed with the appearance
of the place, eligibly located, a gradual descent
from its summit to the margin of the river,
commanding a large commercial business.—
Our steamer being crowded with passengers,
rendering it somewhat inconvenient, especially
to those on the lower deck ; one of the unpleasant features to some of those on the lower
deck who had agreed to perform certain duties
as a part of compensation for their passage,
was by taking in a supply of wood for the
steamer ; this sort of work was necessarily repeated frequently, no matter how cold the
weather was, or what time of night it might
be, the boatmen saluted these men in a loud,
rough tone of voice, " wood! wood! turn out."
If the incumbent was not forthcoming instant-
ly, he might be handled roughly. Without
exception, these river boatmen on the Ohio and
Mississippi rivers are the roughest class of men

that I had ever met with, fearing neither man, law, nor gospel. One of our party became involved in a serious difficulty with these boatmen.

At the expiration of eight or ten days we arrived at the mouth of the Ohio river, being ten hundred and four miles from Pittsburgh. At the confluence of the Ohio and Mississippi rivers is situated the little town of Cairo, noted as a central point for the reconstruction of our army and navy during the great civil war of four years duration. A good specimen of the southern chivalry came under my notice while passing up the Mississippi river, noted for their dueling and gambling propensities; but they have lived to be better and wiser men, brought to their sober senses by a bitter experience of their own folly.

Our little steamer floated upon a favorable current of water upon the Ohio river, but when she came in position to stem the strong current of the Mississippi river rendering it a test question whether she would be able to stem the current or not; and there are those miserable snags, being a hindrance to our progress.—

While taking a nap upon the upper deck, at night, one or two unnatural revolutions brought me to my wakeful senses, convincing me that the boat had struck a snag, but passing on without receiving any serious injury. It is estimated that no less than eleven hundred lives are lost annually upon the Mississippi River by steamboat explosions, and by running upon snags. The water in the Mississippi River being a thick sediment, a yellowish clay color, its frequent use by the passengers frequently incurs a disease of the stomach and bowels resulting in a serious form. At intervals we witnessed elevations of land on the Missouri side of the river, known as the Missouri Bluffs, while on the other side of the river, in the State of Illinois being a level surface known as the American bottoms, a portion of which being inundated with water.

By slow degrees our little craft tugged along up the river until we arrived at St. Louis, one hundred and seventy-two miles from the mouth of the Ohio River. A large number of steamers were lying at the docks. I was taken by surprise to find such a large commercial interest upon the Mississippi river; St. Louis being eligibly located, containing about ten thousand inhabitants. Since that period it has increased ten fold, correspondingly in keeping with a large portion of the western towns and cities, which grow up like mushroons as it were. Immediately in the rear of the city stretched out a large extent of prairie lands, with a sprinkling of cultivated farms. We were obliged to remain at this place for a period of one or two days, waiting for a passage up the river. After leaving St. Louis, while passing up the river, a shower of rain and wind struck the vessel broadside, rendering her safety somewhat critical.

Arriving at Alton in safety, being twenty-two miles from St. Louis, from thence our journey was continued up the Illinois River, the water being perfectly clear, the thick sediment of the Mississippi River had disappeared, being the drainage of the Missouri River. The surface of the country upon the banks of the Illinois River being somewhat broken with timber and prairie lands, we finally arrived at Pekin, a small village located on the east bank of the river, one hundred and forty miles from Alton. This being the end of our journey by steam power we were obliged to seek some other kind of conveyance to convey us thirty-five miles in the interior of the country. Within a brief period of time my friends had secured teamsters for transporting our personal effects, goods and chattles. After some delay, incurred by loading up our baggage, we started off on our journey, some of our party seated on trunks and baggage, while others went on foot. We found the roads in bad condition, and the country thinly populated, not unusual for the nearest neighbors to be from two to five and ten miles apart, the farmers residing in log cabins built without much simmetry or form, but comfortable, usually containing one room, the crevices between the logs filled in with mud, the chimney on the outside, the floors rough planks, with the entire absence of carpets, not unusual for the mud to be half an inch thick upon the floor, owing to the nature of the soil and the habits of the people. Passing through the little village of Tremont, with its bright shining cottages, reminding us of a New England town, being so dissimilar to the rudely constructed log cabins, it seemed homelike, being the improvements of genuine Yankees, renowned for their productions of enterprise.

After leaving Tremont our journey was continued until after sunset. We put up at a farmer's house, located upon the prairie adjacent to the timber land, being a log cabin containing one room. Our party consisted of eight in all, including the farmer's family, being a large number to stow away in one room of limited capacity ; but yet, under all these unfavorable circumstances this plain, honest hearted man extended the hospitalities, such as he possessed, to the use of our party, a band of weary pilgrims. When the hour of retirement came, rendering a little tight squeezing, but no grumbling, partitions made of sheets and blankets, western fashion, retiring upon the soft side of a rough plank for my bed, all the worldly cares of pleasure and trouble past away into sweet slumbers of rest, the spirit of my dreams was aroused by a quivering sound, the barking of prairie wolves, preventing me from enjoying a good night's rest, and no thanks to the impetuous animals. Our fare being correspondingly in keeping with the place, plain and simple, composed of corn bread, fat pork and potatoes, the real substantials of life. The chimney built upon the outside affording an opportunity to take it in when it rains, and the money currency being so different from that of the State of New York, a five cent piece, by the name of picayune, puzzling one's wits to know whether it was something that grew upon trees, a thing to eat, or of currency ; but the constant drain upon our pockets soon initiated us into the currency of levies, bits, fips, and picayunes, to say nothing of the gold dollars vacating our pockets in no small degree of haste, the suckers never refusing to receive them On the evening of our arrival at this place, being an autumn sky, rendering the scene truly beautiful, reminding us of the oriental sky in the eastern hemisphere. The next day, being a bright clear morning, we set out upon our journey with bouyant spirits, but our journey proved to be a sad experience. At a slow rate of speed, wading through mud and water up to the hubs of the vehicle, we were truly stuck fast in the mud on two or three occasions, our further progress being disputed by the bad condition of the roads, rendering the unpleasant necessity of unloading a portion of our load, and all hands at the wheels, in order to extricate ourselves from our position ; but yet we were more fortunate than many others who are stuck fast in the mud for a period of several days or a week at a time. I thought I had seen bad roads on Long Island, but this far exceeded anything of the kind that I had ever witnessed. During the summer and winter months the prairie roads are usually good, but during the wet season of spring and fall the roads are usually bad.

Two of our party left the wagon and traveled on foot. Arriving at Mackinaw River they were obliged to wade the river up to their armpits by breaking the ice—cold water baptism in the elements of a new country where nature has its free course without being obstructed by bridges.

Arriving at Mackinaw City, a smart little western town, chiefly composed of log cabins, here we added two to the number of our party, a little pet dog by the name of York, and a fine young horse by the name of Kato. At this place I heard some of those famous western stories, that pumpkins grew so large families lived in its shell, and that the citizens had the chills and fever so hard, by leaning up against a tree would shake it down—all true in the time of it.

Our journey was continued until we arrived within a few miles of Bloomington. Here we put up with a farmer located in the woods. Remaining at this place for a period of eight or ten days, the farm house being too small to accommodate the whole of our party, myself and friend took up our lodgings in an humble cot, a small log cabin surrounded by the wilderness, a lonely secluded place, shut out from the busy scenes of the outside world, affording the opportunity for reflection upon the pathway of life, which has its ups and downs, and cannot be avoided. Our journey had been long and tedious, performing a distance of nearly two thousand miles, being associated with some pleasant reflections, while others were sad, it was with regret to learn the death of two young ladies from the State of Connecticut, contributing so much by their social musical powers to wile away our leisure hours pleasantly. One of these young ladies died while on her passage up the Mississippi River, the other within a brief period of time, after arriving in the State of Illinois. Such is the uncertainty of life that we know not the day nor yet the hour when the brittle thread of life will be cut asunder, and cast us into the ever-lasting gulf of eternity. We had not yet arrived to the end of our journey, being thirteen miles to Hudson, the place of our destination.

We left the abodes of our humble cot, to be occupied by crickets, owls and bats, passing through Bloomington, a flourishing little town containing about one thousand inhabitants. From thence, while on our way to Hudson, one of our party shot a prairie rattle snake containing four or five rattles ; under the most favorable circumstances such companions are not desirable pets, although I have seen a young lady on exhibition wind these serpents around her neck, while the sterner sex, my friend, re-pudiated the company of this serpent, and shot him upon the spot. Whether this was an act of cruelty or not I will leave for others to judge.

Arriving at Hudson we found it to be a city of stakes, with the entire absence of a solitary building, my friends having the honor of erecting the first house in Hudson, laboring under great disadvantages, the limited supply of building materials and labor rendering the process of the erection slow and tedious, hauling a portion of their lumber nine or ten miles over bad roads. The completion of the building stands as a monument in commemoration of the enterprise. The first settlers of a new country experience many inconveniences and endure many hardships by erecting houses, building roads and bridges, and clearing up timber lands—they pave the way for their children to enjoy the fruits of their labors. It was not unusual for the farmers to be gone from home eight or ten days to mill, fifteen or twenty miles. These are some of the conditions and facilities to which the inhabitants of a newly settled country are exposed.

Hudson is located upon an open prairie, bounded on the west by timber lands ; here we found located four families, by the respective names of Havens, Smith, Trimmer and Wheeler, well to live, I might say independent farmers, undisturbed by the selfish ambition of wealth and pride, happy aad contented, reminding us of the good olden times in the days in

which our forefathers lived. There is no life
equal to the independent farmer.

> Let sailors sing of the ocean deep,
> Let soldiers praise their armor—
> But in my heart this toast I will keep,
> The independent farmer.

These generous hearted farmers accommo-
dated us with the hospitalities of good board,
but when the hours of retirement came, requiring a large degree of philosophy to be ex-
ercised, and a good share of patience, to facil-
itate matters agreeable to all parties. In order
to relieve these difficulties myself and friend
made a change, by occupying a log cabin two
miles distant from our neighbors, our humble
cot being situated in the woods upon the banks
of the Mackinaw River. Here we kept bach-
elor's hall in a style that might be valuable
lessons to some of the fair sex, although the
simplicity of such a life might bear hard upon
epicurians of gay, fashionable circles. But
as we made no pretensions of show and fashion, we enjoyed the blissful scenes of our humble cot, surrounded by nature's sweetest blessings, in the enjoyment of good health, exhal-
ing a bright pure atmosphere, the gentle winds

discoursing a melody of sweet music through the forest ; the song of the morning lark and the nightingale, as it fell upon our ear, was a source of pleasure.

A home amid the flowers,
Where birds in summer sing,
Has many merry hours—
Naught else from it can spring.

And the quail whistling so sweetly by our cottage door day after day, receiving a visit from the owl and wolf at night. These were our daily and nightly companions. We were surrounded by game, quail, wild turkeys, and prairie hens, gray squirrels, rabbits, wolves, and deer, in large numbers. No less than fifteen deer came under my observation during one afternoon. While in pursuit of them I was led three or four miles into the wilderness. On approaching a small Indian hut I found it vacated—no signs of life—remnants of deers' skins and deers' horns being the only vestige left to adorn the interior of this humble secluded cot, and indeed I had penetrated the wilderness so far it was attended with difficulty to find my way back, the sun being my only guide by calculating the time of day, and its position, enabling me to steer my course in the right direction.

And how solemn are these desolate wildernesses, rippling streams and lisping winds sounding through the forest as if some small still voice was speaking to us, creating a feeling of reverence in the secret chambers of our hearts in acknowledgment of the Creator's omnipresence everywhere, amid the ocean wave, in the deep recesses of the valley, or on the mountain top—we are in the presence of Him that created all things. Century after century has rolled around, and we still find these wandering tribes grovelling their way through the wilderness in darkness without the light of the gospel, in a state of barbarism, subsisting chiefly upon the spontaneous productions of the country, engaged in their wild sports of hunting.

Deer hunts are wild, exciting sports. I was deeply interested in watching the movements of the deer. It is a beautiful sight to witness the deer leaping over creeks, and bounding over hill and dale, with great velocity of speed. While passing through a deep valley in the

woods my attention was suddenly arrested by
the presence of a deer upon the crest of the hill,
passing down the valley in close contact of my
position. As if by magic speed he passed out of
my sight. It was worse than useless for the
bullets in my rifle to make an attempt to follow an animal running with such velocity of
speed. He was quickly followed by an old
huntsman, containing one eye, of dark com-
plexion, resembling the appearance of an Indian. The wild and sudden appearance of
these animals frightened me almost out of my
seven senses—at least quite equal to an electric
shock. On another occasion I became alarmed
at the wild pranks of a buck deer, as if desiring to give me battle. I had secreted myself
in the grass, intently watching the deer feeding in the low grounds of the prairie. Losing
sight of the animal I suddenly arose upon my
feet. At the same instant, within a few yards
of my position the deer leaped several feet
above the high grass, blowing his whistle
through his nostrils, and striking his feet heavily upon the ground. In the glare of sunlight
his eyes shone like two fire balls, resembling
some ferocious animal. These manœuvers being repeated, as if reluctant to leave the spot,

exciting my nervous system to such a degree as to prevent the discharge of my gun.

During the long evenings of autumn, while myself and friend was returning from a visit with our neighbors, while passing through the woods amid intense darkness, we were necessitated to feel our way from tree to tree, and crawl upon a log over a creek. Notwithstanding the intense darkness, we started a deer running through the woods with great velocity of speed, showing the superiority of the sight of the animal to that of man. And the wild turkey was an object of my special attention on one occasion. While a flock of wild turkeys was feeding upon the prairies adjacent to the timber lands, it was my design to get a shot at them ; but the moment my presence became visible to them they took leg bail and ran with such rapidity of speed as to leave me in the back grounds ; by secreting themselves in the woods, not one of them could I discover afterwards. But it was my pleasure to shoot the first wild turkey of our party. After returning home with my prize the voluntary services of our good land lady was brought into speedy requisition, preparing it for roasting.

Our Long Island friends were invited to dine with us ; we enjoyed the hospitalities of a good supper, and the way that my portion of the turkey was demolished was the best evidence in the world that it was well prepared, and of excellent quality. The hours of the evening being wiled away pleasantly by listening to some romantic tales, and the life of the back-woodsman as related by our western friends, was peculiarly interesting. Being in the presence of a sparkling bright fire, added no small degree of interest and cheerfulness to the scene. It was one of those old-fashioned kitchen fire-places, affording ample room for the boys to sit upon the end of the back-log and crack hickory-nuts, reminding us of the good olden times when we were boys. There are incidents in life, however trifling in its nature, are reminiscences never to be forgotten. On the approach of evening the stillness of the hour was broken by the tingling sound of cow bells returning from the boundless fields of the prairies, yielding the dairy maid a bountiful supply of milk and butter. It is not those only that live in palaces that enjoy all the good things of this life ; even those that live in log cabins in the seclusion of the wilderness enjoy the fruits of their labor—the luxury of venison, prairie hen and wild turkey. The prairie hen was exceedingly abundant, frequently rising from the prairies in large numbers, from one hundred to one and two thousand in a flock. Their clucking voices, and the roaring sound of their wings, as they flew, somewhat resembled a tornado of wind. As they arose suddenly the effect was startling. During the white frosty mornings in autumn, large numbers of them came from the prairies and lighted upon the trees and in the corn-fields, affording a fine opportunity for sportsmen. The prairie hen is about the size of a large sized pullet, short legs, plumage dark gray, with a mixture of white, with a topnot upon her crown, entitling her as the queen of the west ; and those noble birds, the sandhill crane, are inhabitants of the prairies during the summer months, where they lay and hatch and rear up their young broods into maturity. Being birds of migration, take flight for more congenial climes during the winter months. And those innocent, beautiful little birds, the quail, were quite abundant. Having a desire to secure two or three of them for my pets, I set myself to work forming a loose out of the hair of a horse's tail. After this work had been completed, the quail being exceedingly gentle, were driven in the snare. Having caught two or three of them alive, they were confined in a cage for my own amusement; but as their companions were frequently heard whistling or calling them, they became restless in their unnatural homes, and as they strove day after day with almost the instinct of human efforts for their liberty, the power of conscience of doing wrong over-balanced the sense of pleasure, induced me to liberate them from their prison cell. It has frequently been a question within my mind whether it is not wrong or sinful to confine birds in a cage for our own amusement. Every living creature seeks for his liberty.

And the large number of gray squirrels was an object of interest for sportsmen during our first experience at hunting. Large numbers were shot by my friends, but we soon discovered that the game was too small for the waste of powder. The family of squirrels are varied in size and color—the gray squirrel, the fox squirrel and the black squirrel, united harmoniously together. The fox squirrel frenquently resting upon the highest branches of the trees,

seemirgiy as if he was a sovereign within himself, out of harms way, saucily laughing or
barking at us diminative looking creatures
below. And those innocent animals, the rab-
bit, frequently fell a pray by the force of the
hunters' bullet.

I have thus extended at some length a min-
ute description of the game in the west, but it
may not be inexpedient to draw a brief sketch
of his lordship, the prairie wolf. I have no
knowledge of his antecedents, whether they
were bears, dogs or wolves, but as we find him
in his present state, he is a source of great an-
noyance to the farmers, very destructive to
sheep. They had the boldness to chase the
sheep up to the door of our cabin in broad daylight. Having no firearms at my command,
the services of the dogs were brought into
speedy requisition, resulting in a contested
race. The wolves, taking the advantage of the
slews, left the dogs in the background to bark
and howl as long as they pleased over the de-
feat. The wolves being unsuccessful in their
attempt by daylight, took the advantage of the
darkness of night by visiting our neighbor's
sheep pen, killing several of his sheep. Hav-

ing a desire that the wolves should pay a penalty for their evil deeds, on the following night we secreted ourselves in ambush, watching for the wolf to make his appearance. Either the instinct of the animal or the sense of smell prevented us from being favored with the presence of such an animal. During the moonlight nights it was my pleasure to set the dogs upon the wolves, but if they were too closely pursued, they would turn upon the dogs, being cowardly would turn tail to and run back nearly as fast as they went. But as poor old "watch" had been seriously injured by the wolves in his youthful days, elicited a large share of sympathy for his cowardice, but there was no excuse for his comrades. The prairie wolf is of a medium sized dog, long tail, sharp nose, dark brown hair, well formed with the exception of his small eyes and sharp nose, rendering a mean appearance characteristic of the animal. During the winter months, when the ground is frozen, the farmers participate in wolf hunting expeditions upon horseback, accompanied by their dogs. In this manner large numbers are slaughtered. The increase of emigration and the progress of civilization drives the game and the Indians back

into the interior of the wilderness. During my
hunting expeditions I frequently came in contact with a large number of hogs in the woods,
feeding upon nuts and acorns. The slightest
noise or shuffling of the leaves was a signal of
alarm. Pricking up their ears with two or
three grunts, would start and run like wild
deers, but the wild boar is a fearful and dangerous animal to come in contact with.

Among the various species of forest trees
was a noble collection of sugar maple trees,
yielding a good supply of maple sugar. Chest-
nut and locust were exceedingly scarce, oak
being more abundant than any other kind of
timber. Pine, cedar and hemlock were among
the things that had no existence. By travelling fifty miles not the slightest resemblance of
an evergreen tree could be seen. Fruit trees,
such as pairs, apples and peaches, grew exceedingly well, yielding a good supply of fruit.
The soil is black, from one to three feet deep,
resting upon a clay bottom. The grass grows
from one to six feet high, being good grazing
lands, the raising of stock, hogs, horses and
cattle, is a great source of revenue to the farmers. The soil is fertile and productive, and

indeed the State of Illinois is one of the first
States in the Union for the production of stock
and grain, especially corn. The farmers frequently plant from fifty to one hundred acres
of corn, even a larger number of acres are
planted. A single field of corn being equal to
a large size farm on Long Island. The surface
is flat with the exception of slight rolling prairies in certain localities. After the prairie
lands are broken, its cultivation is attended
with comparative ease without the excessive
labor of manuring, free from roots or stone.
By traveling fifty miles a stone as large as a
chippy bird's egg could not be seen. The climate is healthy with the exception of chills
and fever, more especially upon the river cour-
ses. It is changeable to excess with wet and
dry weather, heat and cold. The early frost
in Autumn frequently injures the crops of corn.
One of the great draw-backs to the State is
the scanty supply of wood, not more than one
third of the surface being woodland. Myself
and friends having a desire to secure a tract of
woodland, it was involved upon me to perform
the duties of searching out the boundry lines.
Having a late plot from the land office, with
the assistance of a guide, I started upon this

little expedition upon horse-back, fording rivers and exploring the wilderness, over hill and dale, for a period of one or two days. After this work had been completed with some degree of success, preparations were made to go to the land office at Danville to enter the lands. Being one hundred miles, the thinly populated condition of the country, over bad roads, rendering the expedition somewhat unpleasant, especially as it was a strange road to pass over, but the thoughts of fear scarcely entered my mind. The sun had set in the western horizon before returning home from my researches of the boundry lines of timber lands. Having a desire to start early the next morning for the land office, there was no time to be lost in preparing for the journey. The first thing to be looked after was the condition of the horse, being youthful and of a formidable size, rendering her in good condition for the journey, with the exception of being barefooted. It was a happy circumstance of having the will and faculty of making ourselves useful ; a set of rudely constructed tools was brought into speedy requisition within a brief period of time; with a strong nerve and a good share of elbow grease, a set of shoes was nailed upon the animal's feet by candle light. After this portion of the work had been completed the animal was the recipient of a good mess of oats preparatory for the arduous duties about to be performed by her the next day.

The next thing in question came up the important subject—the condition of our finances for defraying our expenses. Nothing but gold and silver were received at the land office for the payment of public lands. A small purse containing a few rusty dollars was carefully examined and counted over. An additional sum being presented to me by my friends, increased its size to a formidable position, being a good prize for highwaymen. A pair of horse pistols was tendered me by my friends for the protection of my person and purse. The arrangements being completed for the journey, I retired for rest and repose. The dogs kept up a furious barking as if some evil designed person might be lurking about the premises, preventing me from enjoying a good night's rest, seemingly as if my money purse began to make me feel a little uncomfortable. Happy is the man whose rest is sweet without being troubled with the filthy lucre.

Our kind landlady, Mrs. Wheeler, arose early and prepared my breakfast at one o'clock in the morning. Being a beautiful moonlight night, the services of my favorite animal was brought into speedy requisition. Mounting my noble steed, off we started, bounding over a ten mile prairie. As I beheld the silvery rays of the moon gleaming over the broad expanse of the rolling prairies, rendering the appearance of the ocean. I had not proceeded on my journey more than four or five miles when the animal started suddenly at full speed for some considerable distance, before I could hold her up.— Gaining self possession of my senses, I looked back, but could discover nothing in the form of an antagonist. I only had a few moments for reflection before the same experiment was repeated, resulting in the same manner as on the previous occasion. I could discover nothing. I was determined, if possible, to discover the secret of these pranks of the animal by holding a taught rein While looking back she started again—this time I beheld a wolf come out of the grass into the road within a few paces of the horse, sufficiently near to shoot with my revolver. Fearing that it might startle the horse, and as I had no desire to

waste my powder and ball, the wolf was un-
molested to pursue his own way, following us
several miles until the dawn of day.

Arriving at Bloomington, halting for a few
moments, from thence our journey was continued a due East course. While crossing a fifteen mile prairie, a thick fog came over the
horizon, resembling the appearance of being
upon mid ocean. A mariner at sea without a
chart or compass to steer his course places him
in an unpleasant position. An imperfect road
being my only guide, a lumbering sound of
thunder indicating that a storm was approaching. It seemed so unnatural, the report being
so sudden and so near the surface, as if it might
be a rupture of the earth. The heavy state of
the atmosphere produced this singular phe-
nomenon. As I was riding along leisurely I
was suddenly startled by the presence of an
object within a few years in advance of my
position resembling the appearance of a man in
a helpless condition ; but it proved to be a
cloak that some person had dropped by the
roadside. I dismounted and secured my prize.
The roads being in such bad condition I was
obliged at intervals to go a quarter of a mile

from the main road to the head of slews.—
While attempting to cross a deep narrow
stream, the horse made a sudden bound,
bringing my head in contact with her rump,
receiving quite an unpleasant sensation, but no
injury. During my second day's journey, while
passing through the woods, it became evident
that a little bitter experience lay in my pathway. Our further progress being disputed by
the bad condition of the road, passing over an
imperfect corduroy road, which are usually bad
roads at best, the horse stumbling and slip-
ping between logs and roots, up to the knee
joint in mud and water, imperiling the danger
of broken limbs. My own safety and sympathy for the animal compelled me to dismount
and lead the animal I performed forty-eight
miles the first day, and forty-five miles the
second day, rendering a tiresome, tedious journey. At nine o'clock on the morning of the
third day I arrived at Danville, entered my
lands and returned on my journey homeward.
At the expiration of five or six days from the
time I left Hudson, I returned in safety with
a due appreciation of the services of Lady
Kate, gliding over the prairies and through the
woods two hundred miles without faltering in

her energies, always ready to obey the word of
command. I became attached to this faithful
animal for her usefulness, beauty, and speed.
It is indeed wicked to treat these noble animals
with cruelty.

> A man of kindness to his beast is kind—
> But brutal manners show a brutal mind ;
> Remember He who made thee made the brute,
> Who gave thee speech and reason made him mute.
>
> He can't complain—yet God's all-seeing eye
> Beholds thy cruelty and hears his cry.
> He was designed thy servant and thy drudge—
> But know that his Creator is thy Judge.

Adjacent to the Southern boundery of Hudson stretched out a wide extent of prairie lands
During the summer months strawberries and
wild-flowers are some of the luxuries that
adorn the landscape of the prairies. The
beauty of prairie roses are familiar plants to
those that have a passion for cultivating flowers.

> The flowers that beautify the earth,
>   And claim our cultivating care,
> A lesson of intrinsic worth,
>   For our instruction hear.

During the fall months the prairies are usually burnt over. A prairie fire at night is one

of the most beautiful scenes in the west, although wild. Sweeping over the prairies with great force, it may be compared to a sea of fire, resembling the sound of the rolling billows of the ocean, moving with such velocity of speed that emigrants have perished in the flames. It has been my privilege, in company with several other persons, to fight these prairie fires a great portion of the night for the protection of timberlands, farms and dwellings. It was attended with excitement and fatigue, the fire driving before it the wild animals and birds, flocks of prairie hens in their flight soaring away above the cloud of smoke for places of security, and the deer in wild amazement bounding over the prairies with great velocity of speed. In the glare of light, the wolves and rabbits fleeing before the flames with all the speed they possessed, with our dogs in pursuit of them, the rabbits being the easiest prey of the chase. The surrounding elements being a glare of light tufts of grass soaring high in the air alighted in flames. Such scenes are decidedly exciting and interesting. But the time had arrived for returning home. I left Hudson and went to Bloomington ; here I remained for a period of eight or ten days, waiting for two

travelling companions to accompany me to the
Eastern States. The weather was exceedingly
cold a portion of the time, the frost forming a
snowy white surface upon the cover lids of my
bed at night. A snow storm was succeeded by
a rain storm—a slush of snow and water pre-
vailed.

While making some additional preparations
for our journey, the expediency of calling upon
a cobbling shoemaker opposite the hotel where
I was boarding was among one of the first
things to be done. While returning, at the instant of placing my feet upon the sidewalk, a
tornado of wind came up out of the west—
boards from a lumber yard flying wild and
high in the air. The moment it struck my
person my hat took a speedy flight, landing
into the bottom of a well. It was undignified
on the part of my hat to forsake my company
in such a style, leaving my head exposed to
the elements, disarranging the locks of my hair
with great confusion. It was attended with
difficulty to keep my equilibrium from being
carried off my feet. Before reaching the opposite side of the street, the snow and ice cracked
under my feet, the surface freezing hard by the

force of the storm as it swept over the horizon. Several persons, horses and cattle, froze to death by the intense severity of the weather. It was the most sudden and severe change that I had ever experienced, being the experience of the oldest inhabitants.

It was my design to return home by the route I came, but as the rivers were frozen over I changed my course and took the overland route through the interior of the States. The next day after Christmas, on the 26th of December, 1836, myself, and two friends by the respective names of Magoun and Foster, started on our journey on foot. More than a thousand miles were to be accomplished—a nice little walk to prepare us for the duties of the breakfast table, requiring some degree of courage to perform the work; but we were going home. The surface being covered with snow and ice, rendering our passage slow and tedious, producing sore feet and stiff limbs. The first night we put up at a farmor's house, one of the farmer's daughters, scarcely out of her teens, of no extraordinary beauty, attracted my special attention. In reply to an inquiry of one of my companions, in the simplicity and awkwardne s of her nature exclaimed: "Mar! Mar! that are feller wants some grease to greaze his boots!" causing one of my companions to bite his lips tightly while the other burst out in a fit of laughter. Turning it off upon some other incident, the young lady never knew that she was the object of our sports. Her exclamation was the event of a bye-word with our party. When one or the other got the blues or dumps, a repetition of her remarks seldom failed to make a favorable impression upon the countenance of the incumbent.

The ladies in the west in those days were downright homemade looking—no artificial fancy fixings to adorn their person. I shall never forget a little incident. When we were travelling upon the crest of a hill there came up from the deep valley sweet tones of music from a lady's voice, echoing through the forest, over hill and dale, in the stillness of a twilight evening, it was enchanting, which seemed to show how happy and contented she was in that secluded, humble cot. Contentment is the secret of happiness in any condition of life.

And now we have enjoyed a good night's

rest, we must prepare for the duties of the second day's journey. A little stiffness of limbs seemed to prevail; brisk rubbing was a better remedy than medicine. At eight o'clock we started upon our journey. During the afternoon, while crossing a wide prairie, I became so much exhausted that it was attended with some uncertainty whether I would be able to reach the next stopping place without the assistance of my companions. The moment I entered the house I threw myself upon the bed without having time to throw off my overcoat. I was completely exhausted. By keeping quiet for a period of half an hour I recovered sufficiently to take my position in front of the fire. My limbs were so sore and stiff that I had not the power to raise them from the hearth without assistance. I began to think that our journey on foot was at an end, my companions having a desire to purchase a horse for my use, but I felt so much better in the morning, I made a proposition to continue our journey on foot, by taking it moderately. This proposition being accepted, we continued our journey until sunset without being exhaused : but I felt the effects of the journey very sensibly, sometimes falling in rear of my companions quite a long distance. On the fourth day of our journey I kept up with my companions. At the expiration of one or two weeks I frequently left them in the rear, stopping at the farmers' houses, feasting upon apples or cider, until they came up. We became so accustomed to walking that we performed about as many miles a day as those upon horseback. On an average we performed a distance of twenty-two miles per day, the fartherest being thirty-three miles. By walking seven miles before breakfast it requires no philosopher to guess that it gave us a good appetite for our breakfast. It was amusing to witness a table full of hungry men demolish a plate of hot cakes. "Hurry up your cakes!" was the trumpet sound falling from the lips of some green Dutchman, without having any degree of sympathy for the plighted haste of the cooks roasting over a hot fire.

Through the country which we had passed in the State of Illinois, being a level surface, chiefly prairie lands, as far as the power of sight could extend over a forty mile prairie, the horizon resembling a vast ocean of sea. Day after day we travelled over these prairies, the cold west wind sweeping over the surface with great force ; frost bitten ears and red noses being an evidence of the cold winds sweeping over the prairies with a resistless force. One of the prettiest prairie scenes, known as the Oasis, small groves of timber looming up over the horizon, resembling pyramids or some distant village or city, and the timber, where the fire had destroyed the vitality of their trunks, standing bleached white with the weather, their branches forming spires and steeples in the glare of sunlight, are scenes peculiarly interesting. But when we passed through the State of Indiana the aspect of the scene changed somewhat, the surface being level, but for the most part heavily timbered. A large portion of their farms are clearings of timber land. The large number of woodpeckers, many of them of beautiful plumage, prosecuted their portion of the work faithfully between the two elements. The wood-pecker and the wood chopper, the trees were felled to the ground, the consuming flames committed them to dust and ashes, the final destiny of all animate and inanimate life. Day after day we witnessed smoke from fires where the farmers were clearing their timber lands. They were painful scenes to witness while reflecting how many poor families are suffering for the want of fuel. During the winter months it seems sinful to destroy such large tracts of valuable timber. It is indeed a hard, laborious way of becoming in possession of farms. Why not prefer the prairie lands, where this kind of labor is not endured. But happily and fortunately for the human race that we do not all feel and think alike, reminding us of the truthfulness of our school-boy rhymes:

> Many men of many minds,
> Many birds of many kinds,
> Many fishes in the sea,
> Many men can't agree.

So it is, and so it always will be. What is one's pleasure is another's misery. The minds of men are as varied as the pebbles upon the sea shore. The surface being level where the roads was cut through the timber on a straight line, an object could be seen seven miles distant. Arriving at Indianapolis, the Capital of the State, we visited the Senate Chamber, then in session. From thence our journey being continued, arriving at Richmond I tarried all night with a Friend by profession. He was formerly a resident of Jericho, Long Island, being one of the early settlers of this place.—

By paying strict attention to his business, in connection with the rise of property, he acquired a fortune.

The next morning, after enjoying the hospitalities of a good breakfast, a plain coach, with a fine team of horses attached, drove up to the door in readiness for a tour of inspection thro' the city. Our ride was extended to the suburbs of the city, visiting a Friends' meeting house of spacious dimensions, a brick edifice. The exterior surface and the interior apartments were finished plain, corresponding with the profession of my friend. I was favorably impressed with the thriving condition of the Friends at this place. After returning home the time had arrived for our last parting farewell. With a grateful remembrance for the kind attention I had received at the hands of my friend. From thence our journey being continued, passing into the State of Ohio, the aspect of the country somewhat changed. The level surface which we had passed over in the States of Illinois and Indiana, terminated with a broken, hilly surface in the western part of the State of Ohio, somewhat mountainous in the eastern part.

While prosecuting our journey through villages and cities, the intense blackness of the buildings of Zanesville attracted my special attention, being exclusively a manufacturing place. Arriving at Columbus, the Capital of the State, we visited the Senate Chamber, then in session. By the kindness of a friend we were permitted to visit the State Prison, a spacious brick building, no less than three hundred convicts confined within its walls, conveying an unfavorable impression for a portion of the inhabitants of the State. We were now on the great national road, being macadamized, rendering fine travelling. I was taken by surprise to find such a large thoroughfare through this Western country. A large number of stages with splendid horses attached. The finest horses in the country are selected for these stage routes, no less than seven stages passing in the same direction between the hours of twelve o'clock and sunset. The mail stages continued to run all night. Where the roads was hilly or mountainous over an icy surface, rendering the passage difficult and dangerous, the drivers frequently run their horses down the mountain. If the slightest accident should occur, might precipitate them over a steep precipice or down the mountain at a fearful rate; if the horses were permitted to walk there was danger of the hind wheels sliding around, and upset the stage. Their speedy flight down the mountain was to prevent such an occurrence, but between the two I would prefer to risk the chances of the slow rate of speed   But even where the surface is level, they drive their horses at a rapid rate of speed, changing horses every eight or ten miles; and as the driver passes over the road a certain number of miles, too and fro, become as well acquainted with the road as a pilot upon a river; and the horses being well trained to their work, less accidents occur than might be expected, the loss of life being proportionately less than upon the steam cars at the present time.   When we approached the city of Dayton, from the crest of a hill, the city laying beneath us with its domes and glittering spires in the gleam of sunlight, was truly a beautiful scene.   Dayton is one of the prettiest cities in the western States, a good business place.   Our journey was continued on foot until we arrived at Elizabethtown, Ohio; here we purchased a horse and jumper, plain and simple in all its arrangements, two sapling poles embracing the runners and shafts, a slight frame work erected for the sides and seat, rope traces and lines, a rope suspended over the horse's back attached to the shafts answering in the place of britchen. This plain, simple fixing attracted the attention of the passers by, especially the boys, desiring to make a little sport over the simplicity of our rudely constructed conveyance ; but as one of my companions always being ready to drop a word in the right place, enabling us to continue on our journey without being molested by the boys. The roads being icy, and the country hilly, rendering our progress slow and tedious, while winding our way up the mountains, the weather being cold, we generally walked up in preference to riding, and indeed, we had become so accustomed to walking, that more than half of our journey was performed on foot, after purchasing the horse. The State of Ohio is one of the finest producing States in the Union, embracing a fine soil, and well timbered. We crossed the Ohio river at Wheeling. The greatest portion of the river had been crossed upon the surface of the ice, while others being crossed upon flat bottom boats, occasionally waiting quite a long time upon the banks of the river for our turns, or for the floating ice to pass down the river ; it was attended with difficulty to cross the Ohio river owing to the strong current and floating ice.

The boundary line of the State of Ohio being situated upon the west bank of the Ohio river, the State of Virginia upon the other, and the boundary line of the State of Pennsylvania being only ten miles from Wheeling, was an event of passing over three boundary lines within a brief period of time. We had now entered the mountainous region of Pennsylvania, famous for its coal mines. Simply out of curiosity we entered one of these coal mines at a considerable distance, passing through an archway dimly lighted up with lamps ; here we beheld a large number of workmen, some were engaged with their pick-axes, while others were wheeling the coal out upon barrows. Being a dark damp place, in connection with a thick dialect of language that we could not well understand, we thought it would be prudent to leave those gloomy abodes with our best wishes that its inmates might enjoy a peace of body and mind ; but as to myself, I would have no desire to drag out a miserable existence in such a damp, dark, gloomy looking place as we witnessed in those coal mines.

Occasionally while passing at the foot of lofty mountains for a succession of hours, or nearly all day, the sun was not visible. Being surrounded by snow and ice, reminded us of being in an arctic region, the mercury ranging a few degrees above zero ; the trees cracking with ice ; at intervals the snow and ice sliding down at the foot of the mountain with a heavy crash ; the cold northwest winds whistling about our ears creating a sort of chills and fever shaking— how cold and dreary are such scenes, as if all nature had yielded to the power and influence of the ice king.

As we beheld the smoke curling from the chimney of some humble cot nestling among the trees in some distant valley, was an evidence that some signs of life existed in these cold dreary solitudes of the wilderness ; and now as we behold the bright rays of the sun rising gradually over the peak of the mountain, stimulates us with new life, our step becomes more elastic. Onward march was our motto and watchword, while winding our way up the mountains ; it was not unusual to perform a distance from two to three miles to attain the summit of the mountain ; while in the valley beneath a landscape of farms, rivers, villages, and cities, was an object of interest; and the dewy vapors of misty fog as it arose from the valley beneath on a bright clear morning as the sun reflected upon its snowy white surface, was peculiarly interesting. Tracing out the line of rivers at a long distance by the fog that arose from its surface, the fog floating along the valley without attempting to make us a visit in the upper regions of snow and ice. The dewy ice drops forming diamonds and spangles in the glittering sunlight of a cold frosty morning, crystalizing the forest with robes of beauty, are scenes of no small degree of interest, reminding us that beauty existed in a state of dreariness, and comfort in a state of poverty; and the peculiarity of the forest trees being an object of interest; white pine, hemlock, and the mountain pine were some of the varieties of the forest scenery. We found a great thorough-fare crossing over the mountains by wagons loaded with flour from Pittsburgh to Philadelphia. The idea of carting flour four hundred miles over a mountainous country by wagons, seems almost incredible in these fast days of steam power and electricity; but yet it was done on a large scale, being the only means of transportation during the winter months, and indeed it was decidedly interesting to witness the intelligence of the animals. By proper training one rein answering the purpose for four or six horses, two abreast. In some instances no reins at all, being governed by the word "hoop," "hoy," and "gee." But the wheel horses had the burden of the labor in holding back while going down the mountain, not unusual for them to slide along upon their feet, and the wheels sliding upon the icy surface, rendering the transportation of these wagons difficult and unsafe, where there are so many steep precipices, occasionally tumbling down the precipice at a fearful rate. The horses are large and powerful, a four horse team drawing a burden from three to four tons weight. The wagons are built large and strong, containing a canvass top stretched over hoops or poles, each wagon being furnished with a heavy brake or lock to prevent them from making a speedy flight down the mountain. Their progress up the mountain being at a slow rate of speed, stopping at intervals for rest, performing a distance from fifteen to twenty miles per day. The teamsters are usually a hardy rough class of men, mostly German. Some of the villages and farming districts are almost exclusively German, many of them possess splendid farms. In some instances their farms would cost from two to three thousand dollars, while their houses would be small tenements, a log cabin. On each succeeding day we steadily pursued our journey over the icy surface of mountains and valleys, crossing the Susquehanna river upon the surface of the ice at Harrisburg. While on our tour West we followed the trail of the Susquehanna river a long distance: it was a beautiful sight to witness the varied forms of that noble river winding its way through mountains, rocks, hill and dale, sometimes expanding into pools or lakes, at other times a narrow turbulent stream ; sometimes bold and deep, at other times shallow, forming cataracts, the water tumbling headlong over steep precipices, dashing against the rocks with its snowy white foam in connection with the banks of the river, being draped with the beautiful foliage of evergreen trees and shrubbery, rendering it a picturesque scene. On our return, arriving at Harrisburg the Capital of the State, we visited the Senate Chamber, then in session. From thence our journey being continued, crossing the Delaware river at Easton, passing into the State New Jersey, arriving at Morristown, the Capital of the State, we visited the Senate Chamber, then in session. It was our pleasure to visit the Capitals and Senate Chambers of four States : Indianapolis, the State of Indiana; Columbus, the State of Ohio; Harrisburg, the State Pennsylvania; and Morristown, the State of New Jersey. The traveling being in bad condition, a composition of slush and snow, one of our companions, Mr. Foster, purchased a saddle and rode upon horseback, while myself and my other companion Mr. Magoun, for the first time since the commencement of our journey, took a public conveyance. The co-partnership of our horse and jumper terminated at this place. It was difficult to shed a single tear for the parting of our jumper, but take the last parting farewell of our beautiful iron grey pony, who had served us so long and so well, always ready to obey the word of command, being kind and gentle, won the esteem of our friendship with a deep feeling of sympathy for him as a pet and traveling companion. But the time had come when the best of friends must part, whether it be horses or men, perhaps never to see each other again. The kind attention I

had received from my companions during our
journey strengthened the ties and bonds of
friendship, one to the other. Our journey was
attended with exposure, mingled with fatigue
and pleasure, the fond recollections of many little incidents and reminiscences never to be forgotten.

By traveling through the interior of the
States, affording us a good opportunity to witness the general position of the country, of soil
and climate, rivers and lakes, valleys, wood-
lands and mountains. During a period of forty
days we put up with strangers every night.
We found the people well disposed, kind and
accommodating; our food being plain and
substantial, our bills of fare for supper, lodg-
ing and breakfast being from thirty-six to seventy-five cents. The low rates of fare in those
days, compared with the high rates of fare at
the present time, are more than treble. And
now, since our bills of fare have been carefully
examined and settled with the landlord, we are
ready to continue our journey. A coarse
voice and a sharp crack of the whip brought
up a team of horses at the door, attached
to a public conveyance. At the next

moment we found ourselves snugly seated in
an old fashioned top sleigh, crowded with passen
gers, scarcely having elbow room to turn to
the right or the left, with the privilege of see
ing daylight through the ventilating recesse
of the stage, at the risk of being upset at any
moment. Our change of conveyance being from
better to worse, but we were resolved to bear i
without grumbling. We were traveling upon
the sacred soil of New Jersey roads. Dis
tances had been counted by the hundred miles
but now they were counted by the mile ap
proaching the termination of our journey, an
object so desirable, seemingly as if the horse
made double quick time for our special benefit
Arriving at Newark at seven o'clock in the
evening, remaining all night, our journey be
ing continued the next day, arriving in New
York City, on the fifth day of February. 1837
being the fortieth day of our journey, super
ceding the time of a journey to Europe and
back again. What was remarkable, th
weather was clear and cold, the wind from the
west during the whole passage with the excep
tion of a slight snow storm at night, we were
not detained a single day on account of bad
weather. The distance of our journey per

formed on foot being about six hundred miles.
I never enjoyed better health than the day I
arrived home.

What a change of progression has been
wrought over the face of the country since
that period of time. The distance which took
us forty days to perform is performed by steam
power within the same number of hours, and
by telegraph communication within the brief
period of a few seconds. The busy bustle of
villages and cities are located upon the spot
which was a desolate howling wilderness, the
barren wilderness has been made to yield her
increase, the broad expanse of the prairie lands
yielding her abundant crops of harvest. The
cradle and nursery of the world, the great
Mississippi valley, possessing a variety of soil
and climate through which the Mississippi river
winds its way, bearing upon its bosom the
productions of untold wealth. Extending to
the Rocky Mountains, possessing inexhaustable
resources of mineral treasure, our boundary
lines extending from the frozen zones of Oregon
to the purple, flowery banks of Mexico: from

the Pacific to the Atlantic Oceans; the smiling evidence of thrift and industry can be seen in the valleys and upon the hill sides, extending over this broad domain of territory. The brave men of the West and East poured out their blood and treasure freely to preserve this priceless heritage bequeathed to us by our forefathers. The great civil war of America was such as the world had never witnessed, resulting in the emancipation of slavery, with a new era dawning upon our National existence, we can justly claim the proud title of being a free Republican form of government; united we stand a Union of States, one and inseparable. Our power and our influence is acknowledged and felt by all the civilized nations of the earth. The world has never witnessed such a progress of commercial and agricultural interest of wealth and enterprise as exhibited by the United States of America.

Our forefathers gave us liberty, but little did they dream
Of the grand results to follow in this mighty age of steam.
With the march of education this world is set on fire—
We knit our thoughts together with a telegraph wire;
From the Red Sea to the Pacific Ocean,
The telegraph wire is put in motion.

The brief period of ten minutes it only requires
To convey the news ten thousand miles over the wires.
The world is indebted to the energies of our noble Field,
The great telegraph champion of America.

Those who have immortalized their names
as public benefactors for the benefit of the human race are held sacred to the memories of
the people.

What a hero from the battle strife with palms of victory
    crowned,
Forms clarion music in his ear from earth's remotest bound,
What ruler over a nation's love in majesty sublime,
The first, the greatest in the realm, a king in freedom's
    clime,
Return to rural haunts to watch a blessed gladness
In his heart, and that glory is never gone.

Who amid his acres broad and green whose ploughshares
    break the sod,
Prefers in sylvan toils to walk in nature and with God ;
There was but one who retired from conquest, power and
    pride,
For which ambition hath so oft in madness striven and
    died,
There was but one dost ask his name, 'neath fair Virginia's
    sky ;
Go find Mount Vernon's sepulchre, and heed its answering
    sigh.

Of all the spots associated with the history
of this Country, Mount Vernon is the most in-

teresting and attractive, at least such was the
impression made upon my mind. It is impos-
sible to imagine the joy and sadness that awak-
ens the impulses of those who have a heart to
feel, and a mind to appreciate past events which
are brought up vividly before your mind as
you behold the old homestead and tomb of
George Washington, the father of our Country.
Mount Vernon is situated upon the west bank
of the Potomac river, fifteen miles from Washington City. The house is beautifully located
on an eligible point of land, rendering a fine
view for many miles both up and down the noble Potomac river. The old mansion is of
wood, two stories and atic, the ancient architectural style of the house renders it a little
dutchified in appearance, the eves of the roof
extending over the piazza. The house is ninety
feet front, with a two story portico extending
the entire length, from which a fine view may
be obtained over the surrounding country to
the extent of fifteen or twenty miles. The Capitol and some portions of Washington City may
be seen from this position. The portico also
affords a good promenade, a wide hall running
through the centre of the building, with two
spacious rooms on either side of the hall, with

a library room attached, which remains very much the same as when occupied by Washington himself.

Along the walls of the rooms hang engravings which were mostly hunting pieces. Among them may be noticed an engraving of Bunker Hill. The trees which surround the house are quite numerous; and those which are known to have been planted by Washington have been carefully preserved, and are objects of interest, from the seeds of which I have a tree growing in my garden, in commemoration of its origin, and founder of the American Republic. In the rear of the mansion is a spacious lawn, a garden, and two green-houses. About five rods in front of the house, near the river, a little on the angle, is situated the old tomb of Washington, which he built before his death for his remains to be placed in. In the year 1836 a new family vault being erected, the remains of Washington was removed to the new vault. It is situated upon a side hill, the main portion of the vault is composed of brick, the front is marble, a large passage way extending to the tomb, being enclosed with a high iron railing. Within this enclosure two sarcopha-

gus are placed in full view. The one representing Washington is wrought with the arms
of his country by his side. In a corresponding
tomb are the remains of Martha, Consort Washington. The front of the vault is about twelve
feet high by twenty feet wide, and thirty feet
in length. The rear part of the top is even
with the surface of the ground, it is covered
with vines and shrubbery. The tomb and the
house, in fact the whole premises, are visited
with much curiosity, and a deep, heart felt interest by thousands of citizens annually.

The Potomac river is the boundary line between the States of Virginia and Maryland. On
the opposite side of the river, on an angle from
Mount Vernon, may be seen Fort Washington.
This is a considerable fortress, commanding
the whole river. Mount Vernon was named
after the famous Admiral Vernon, under whom
Lawrence Washington had served. This estate
was inherited to George Washington by his
brother Lawrence Washington; but after Geo.
Washington's death it fell into the hands of
John Augustine Washington, under whose care
the place was much neglected. Almost everything had the appearance of decay. But re-

cently it has been purchased by a committee
of ladies, by the contributions of citizens, under
whose supervision at present it is held. Through
the patriotic efforts of the ladies much credit
is due for this noble work. The sacred resting-
place of such a hero, and the homestead of
such a patriot, should ever be preserved from
falling into the ruthless hands of speculators.
This farm originally contained thirteen thousand acres. Since Washington's death it has
been reduced to twelve hundred and fifty
acres. It formerly extended eight miles along
the banks of the Potomac River. The City of
Alexandria is situated on the Northern extrem-
ity, which was once the farm of Washington ;
and even the old church at Alexandria, which
Washington was formerly in the habit of at-
tending, is visited with much curiosity, his
pew being formerly No. 22, on the left hand
isle of the church, which almost every visitor
embraces the opportunity of seating themselves
in this pew just as if an inspiration still lin-
gers in everything that Washington once possessed. So much had Washington gained the
confidence of his countrymen, that what he
said and did was law and gospel. Nations
knew him to be great, but knew not half the

worth that lay concealed beneath his modest
life. Monuments have been erected in some of
the leading cities to his name and fame. The
City of Washington is called as it is with his
name—the seat of Government was a spot that
he loved so well and served so truly—there is
the appropriate spot where the summer sun-
beams linger, and where the breeze from the
blue hills of his own native and beloved Virginia delights to play.

He had always shown himself equal to every
case of emergency as a soldier, and as a statesman ; and he had always been ready to con-
tribute a portion of his means when circumstances required it, and was ready to render
his services when the country demanded them ;
but after performing all that he did, farming
seemed to be his chief enjoyment, where he
could be clustered around his own happy fire
circle at Mount Vernon.

During the winter months he devoted two or
three days in the week to hunting. He kept a
register of his horses and hounds, in which
might be found the names, ages and marks of
each. He was always superbly mounted. He

wore a blue coat, scarlet waistcoat, buckskin breeches, yellow-top boots and velvet cap, and, with his long whip in hand, took the field at daybreak. Will Lee, his huntsman, and a brave array of friends and neighbors frequently followed in the train, but none rode more gallantly in the chase, or with more cheering voice, which awoke the echoes of the woodland, than the host of Mount Vernon. He was one of the accomplished cavaliers; he rode with ease, elegance and power; and, indeed, with his sinewy frame and iron muscle, he had such a tenacious grip with his knees, that a horse might as easily throw off his saddle as such a rider. He would throw himself almost at full length on the animal, with a French horn at his back, and his spurs in flank, this bold rider would rush at full speed through broken or tangled wood in a style at which modern hunters would stand aghast. He rode gaily up to his dogs— nor did he spare his impetuous steed; he never yielded to no man the honor of the brush.

Washington's last hunt with his hounds was in 1785. His time was too much absorbed in his private affairs and public business to allow him to indulge in the field sports, and his fond-

ness for agricultural pursuits induced him to
give away his hounds and take a final leave of
the chase.

He then formed an extensive deer park below the mansion house. At first he stocked it
only with the native deer, to which was added
afterwards the English fallow deer. The stock
increased very rapidly ; but though always
herding together, there never was a perceptible
feature of the slightest mixture of the two races. On the decay of the paling fence the deer
dispersed and herded about the estate. As
many as fifteen or twenty could be frequently
seen in a herd.

The last days of Washington were devoted
to constant and useful employment on his farm.
After the active exercise of the morning in attention to agricultural and rural affairs, in the
evening came the post bag, loaded with letters,
newspapers and pamphlets. His correspondence
was immense, but it was promptly and fully
attended to. No letter was unanswered—this
he deemed a grave offence against good man-
ners and propriety. General Lee once observed
to the Chief : "We are amazed, sir, at the

vast amount of work that you accomplish."—
Washington replied : "Sir, I rise at four
o'clock, and a great deal of my work is done
while others are asleep."

In personal appearance Washington was har-
monious in proportion ; rather spare than full
during his whole life, although his weight was
from 210 to 220 pounds, in his prime. He
stood six feet two inches. His physical strength
was remarkable. In athletic exercises he had
no equal. He was a devoted Christian—a
statesman—and as a military chieftain he had
no superior.

The immortal name of Washington swells
the bosom of every American citizen with en-
thusiastic pride. He was first in war—first in
peace—and first in the hearts of his countrymen.

Our patriot Father and our Country's Sire—
The undying influence of thy sacred name—
Which kindles anew in every heart that fire
Which warms devotion by its genial flame.

Whose generous mind glowed with noble zeal—
Who lived not only for the country's weal—
Not only lived that tyrants might cease,
But lived for Heaven and sought the favor of His face.

Washington City being the seat of Government, and its surroundings, renders it the most interesting city in the United States to visit. The stranger would be amply paid by a visit at the City of Washington. The magnitude and importance of the Government buildings are worthy of special notice, being twenty one in number. The Capitol, the Executive Mansion, the Post-Office, the Patent Office, the Pension Office, the Department of State, the Treasury, Survey Department, the War Department, the Navy Department, Department of the Interior, the office of the Attorney-General, the Arsenal, the Navy Yard, the Observatory, the Smithsonian Institute, the National Medical College, the Columbian College, the Monastery, the Treasury Building, the National Institute, and the City Hall: all of which are spacious buildings. The Capitol is a citadel within itself, surpassing all other buildings of the kind in the world for its beauty and size, covering an area of several acres of ground. The building is chiefly composed of stone and marble, being eligibly located, affording a fine view over the city and surrounding country, including the heights of Georgetown, the windings of the Potomac river, and the city of Alexandria. The city of Baltimore, forty-two miles distant, may be seen from its dome. The erection of this building was commenced in the year 1793; it has been re-modeled to its present completion, at the cost of two or three millions of dollars, comprising four wings, and a large dome in the centre, and a flat dome on each wing, containing a large number of rooms. The Senate Chamber is in the second-story of the North wing, of a semi-circular form, seventy-five feet long and forty feet high. The Hall of Representatives is also in the second-story of the South wing, ninety-six feet long and sixty feet high. The Capitol is surrounded with twenty-four columns of variegated Potomac marble, surmounting a base of free-stone. The Rotunda occupies the centre, and is ninety-six feet in diameter, and the same number of feet high. The room, in its circuit, is divided into eight panels, intended for paintings. The sound of one's voice echoes through the Rotunda as if the presence of a second person was speaking to you, creating a peculiar sound.

The Congressional Library is one of the attractions of the Capitol, containing fifty thousand volumes. The sum of five thousand dollars is annually appropriated by Congress for miscellaneous books.

The President's room is the largest and best furnished in the Capitol, decorated with beautiful paintings.

In addition to the rooms specified, there are also a large number of ordinary, but well furnished, apartments, which are occupied by the Vice President, the Speaker of the House, and other officers, postmasters, Congressmen, and the Committees of the two Houses.

The perusal of a few hours through the interior of this building would be interesting and profitably spent by the stranger.

The surroundings of the Capitol grounds contain thirty acres, enclosed by an iron railing. The Capitol is situated on the western portion of this plat, the grounds being kept in the very neatest of order, consisting of one of the most popular and pleasant resorts for promenading to be found in the metropolis, adorned with a great variety of forest and ornamental trees, fountains and basins of pure water, filled with a variety of fish, including the gold fish, lends an enchantment to the scene. The grounds are represented by a number of species of statuary, the most attractive specimen being a statue of Washington, occupying the centre of the square, East of the Capitol.

Near the western entrance to the Capitol stands a monument, erected by the officers of the navy to the memory of their brother officers, who fell in the war with Tripoli. It is marble, rises out of a pool or basin of water, is forty feet high, and surmounted by an eagle.

The Executive Mansion, or, the President's house, is a splendid building. The corner-stone of this building was laid on the 13th of October, 1792. Being partially destroyed during the last war, it was re-built in 1815. It is situated at the West end of the city, at the intersection of Pennsylvania, New York, Connecticut and Vermont avenues. It occupies the centre of a plat of ground containing twenty acres, and at an elevation of forty-four feet above the waters of the Potomac. The grounds lying South of the mansion have been transformed into a magnificent park. which affords a fine carriage drive three or four miles. The mansion is one hundred and seventy feet front and eighty-six feet deep, built of white free-stone. The front is ornamented with a lofty portico of four Ionic columns; the steps landing upon a broad platform at the entrance of the front door, containing a large number of rooms, elegantly furnished. Directly in front of the mansion the eye rests upon the statue of Thomas Jefferson. A little on an angle, in the centre of La Fayette square, is the statue of General Jackson. It is bronze, and was cast from certain cannon captured by General Jackson in some of his military engagements.

The Patent Office is a spacious building, of Grecian architecture, containing a great variety of American and foreign specimens of art, and of natural history, comprising a museum of the National Institute and Library of some five thousand volumes. In the second story of the building are the invaluable relics of Washington, including his camp-chest, the original Declaration of Independence, the gifts presented from time to time to the Government by foreign powers; Franklin's printing press; a collection of Indian portraits; the treasures of the National Institute; interesting memorials of the late James Smithson; and the extensive treasures secured by the United States Exploring

Expedition under Captain Wilkes. In the first story of the building are collected all the models of machines which have been patented since the foundation of the Government.

The perusal of the interior of this building is interesting and instructive. It is one of the most extensive buildings, and the greatest place of resort, in the City of Washington. The National Cemetery, Georgetown College, Force's Library, the Long Bridge, the Aqueduct, and the Washington Monument, are all objects of interest.

The City of Washington is located upon a level surface, at the confluence of the West and East branches of the Potomac river. The buildings are chiefly composed of brick, well represented with churches, including several first-class hotels. The limits of the city cover an area of ground extending four miles and a half from northwest to southeast, and about two miles and a half from East to West, terminating with the heights of Georgetown, and the Potomac river, with its sloping hills, known as the Arlington heights. A portion of the avenues are laid out in triangular forms, representing fifteen States, which were first to enter the

Union; Pennsylvania avenue being the largest and most beautiful in Washington City, being wide and straight, extending one mile in length, commencing at the West front of the Capitol and terminating at the East front of the Treasury Department.

During the month of May, 1865, it was my pleasure to witness the grand armies of Grant and Sherman pass through this avenue, containing two hundred thousand men, occupying two days for these armies to pass. As hour after hour rolled on, I could scarcely realize where this great mass of human beings came from, but they still kept coming, being from fifteen to twenty abreast, performing a rate of speed of about four miles per hour. Such an army would extend about eighty miles in length. Language cannot express the magnificence of such a grand military display, which may be only witnessed once in a life-time. It was a beautiful sight to witness this army performing double-quick time with the long line of bayonets glittering in the sun-light. The army was composed of infantry, artillery and cavalry, from the first officer in rank down to the wood-chopper, being a composition of races, languages and colors. Grant's army made a splendid appearance in well dressed uniforms, but those of Sherman's army were the hardest and roughest looking set of men that I had ever witnessed; they bore evident signs of the hardships that they had endured during their long marches through the dismal swamps of Georgia and South Carolina; they had shown themselves equal to the task—a band of heroes. The sharp-shooters, bummers, wood-choppers and the slaves marched side by side, and the worn-out mules and horses, corresponding with the men in appearance, carrying a burden of all sorts of war implements and cooking apparatus. Dogs, wolves, foxes, bears, raccoons, owls, hawks, eagles and roosters, being a part and parcel, as trophies of the army. Little negro girls seated on mules, clasping dolls in their arms, apparently as contented and happy as though they were at home; stalwart negroes astride of asses; ladies of fashionable circles participated in the parade, on horseback, while others wore emblems of military attire. The rear was brought up with camels, mounted by negroes. This put a climax to the scene, rendering the appearance as if Africa had been transferred to our shores to assist us in the struggle for liberty. Such a

composition and mixed up state of things is not
seen in our daily walks—a composition of the
great American family, independent within themselves; conquer or die is the motto inscribed
upon their banners. Long lines of banners
floated on the breeze, some were in good condition, while others were shattered with bullets
or worn out with hard service. Many touching
incidents came under my notice; mingled with
joy and sadness by greetings and weepings for
the reception or loss of friends. It was painfu
to witness many of those poor fellows, half clad
bare-footed and care-worn, as if they had lost
the last friend on earth. But the reviving in
fluences of this grand army was greeted with
a hearty welcome by a hundred thousand Amer
ican citizens; the welkin was made to ring by
thousands of cheerful voices, by the tune of old
John Brown.

This grand American army was such as the
world had never witnessed, and I trust will
never have an occasion to witness again; no
for its magnificence, but for the desolating
effects of war. On the preceding day to the
army marching through the city, the two armie
broke up their old camp grounds in the State

of Virginia. I took my position on Capitol Hill, one mile East of the Capitol, to witness the arrival of the army. Long lines of army wagons passed through the city nearly all day. At an early hour in the afternoon the main army came up; regiment after regiment passed by and took up their respective positions upon the surface of an extended plain, well adapted for the occasion. Regiment after regiment formed in long lines, while others formed in hollow squares; the sweet tones of national airs emanating from the numberless brass bands; the display of flags and the movements of the army were an imposing sight. Each regiment in turn came to the ground rest, stacked their arms and pitched their tents, resembling a city of tents of no small magnitude.

While gazing upon this vast multitude of human beings, not a solitary familiar face could I recognize, until Capt. Romer came up and took his position upon the field. It was a pleasant thought that Flushing was so well represented in the great struggle for human liberty and the preservation of the Union. It would be doing injustice to Capt. Romer, if I did not give him credit for the fine condition of his men, horses and battery; the good discipline that they were under seemed to show that he was master of the position he held as commander of the battery.

On the approach of evening I retired from the field and returned to the city. On the two following days, after the army had passed through the city, I took my position at the entrance of Long Bridge, to witness the passage of the army over the bridge. A pontoon-bridge had been thrown over the upper branch of the Potomac river. The entire length of these two bridges was filled with infantry, artillery, cavalry and army wagons, approaching the opposite side of the river. The last vestige of these two armies gradually disappeared, winding their way among the blue hills of Virginia, until nothing of the army could be seen, except a cloud of dust rising above the hills, fading away in the twilight of a western horizon.

These two armies had done a great work; it was with proud satisfaction that they had conquered the enemy, and returning home to rest from their labors, to enjoy the happy fire circles of their friends and families.

At the commencement of this narrative it was my design to confine my remarks chiefly to my expedition through the Western States; but, as a matter of record, I have drawn a brief sketch of Mount Vernon, Washington City, and the grand Military Parade, commanded by Grant and Sherman, two of the most scientific military chieftains of the age; being instrumental in restoring peace and preserving the union of States.

Honor to whom it doth belong,
Let error sink in error's night;
'Tis just that we condemn the wrong,
'Tis just that we reward the right.

And now, since peace has been restored, and the dark, stormy clouds of war swept away from the land, with its commercial and agricultural resources in a prosperous condition, as a nation, we have great cause to feel thankful for the blessings we enjoy under the protecting care of a beneficent, over ruling Providence.

His providence unfolds the book,
And makes his counsels shine,
Each opening leaf and every stroke,
Fulfils some great design.

THE END.

The first gun fired from Fort Sumter, April 13th, 1861, inaugurated the civil war in America, which continued a period of four years, until April 5th, 1865 ; the estimated strength of the Union army being from ten to twelve hundred thousand men ; the loss of life being from two to three hundred thousand. The war was brought to a successful termination, under the executive department of Abraham Lincoln, President of the United States. He was assassinated on the night of April 15th, 1865, by J. Wilkes Booth. The event caused a profound sensation to spread over the land like wild fire. The funeral services were attended with an outburst of grief and mourning throughout the country. Abraham Lincoln was born February 12th, 1809, in Hardin county, Kentucky. He died on the 16th of April, 1865, being fifty-six years, two months and seven days old.

The National debt inaugurated during the war being from two to three hundred thousand trillions of dollars, a very large per centage in comparison to the debt inaugurated during the revolutionary war, under the command and supervision of General Washington, the country being in its infancy and limited in the resources *of* men and money. The account kept by Washington with the United States commenced in June, 1775, which he continued in his own hand writing, with remarkable precision and order, until June, 1783, a period of eight years. A balance was then due him of £1,972 9s 4d, which was admitted by the Government in 1784. When the revolutionary storm was rising, George Washington was sent from Virginia, a delegate to the Continental Congress. In that body he was nominated by John Adams, of Massachusetts, for Commander-in-Chief of the American forces. The nomination was unanimously approved by the members, both from the East and South. He accepted the appointment, and immediately left his home and proceeded to Cambridge, where he took charge of the army and issued his first order in July, 1775, a few days after the battle of Bunker's Hill.

In 1789, the unanimous election of General Washington the first President, and his taking the oath of office on the piazza of the Federal Hall, in Wall street, New York, on the site of the Custom House. .

George Washington being the founder of our

republic, and the father of our country, after serving his country with unparalleled devotion through the trying perils of eight years' war, he refused to receive any compensation for his services, or exclusive honors for himself and family. He was born February 22d, 1732; died December 14th, 1799, being sixty-eight years, nine months and twenty days old.

George Washington and Abraham Lincoln are held in the estimation of the people as the father and savior of our country.

www.ingramcontent.com/pod-product-compliance
Lightning Source LLC
Chambersburg PA
CBHW020307090426
42735CB00009B/1251